Twitter Marketing Unlocked

A Twitter guide to help you connect, communicate, and collaborate successfully to grow your brand or small business.

Angela Hemans

Copyright © 2018 by Angela Hemans. All rights reserved.

Published by Hemans Marketing Media, Georgia, USA

No part of this publication may be reproduced, in any form or by any electronic or mechanical means including information storage and retrieval systems except in the case of brief quotations for articles or reviews- without permission in writing from its author or publisher.

This publication is designed to provide accurate and authoritative information in regards to the subject matter cover. It is so with the understanding that the publisher is not engaged in rendering legal, accounting, or other professional services. If legal advice or other expert assistance is required, the services of a competent professional person should be sought.

The advice and strategies contained and this book may not be suitable for your situation. Neither author or publisher shall be liable for any loss of profit or any other commercial damages including but not limited to special, incidental, consequential, other damages.

ISBN-10: 1724789384
ISBN-13:978-1724789389

DEDICATION

This book is dedicated to everyone who has supported me on this journey. To have you as a part of my life has been a true blessing!

Table Of Contents

Introduction	**8**
Module 1	**10**
Creating The Foundation	**10**
Chapter 1	
Introducing your business brand and Understanding your purpose for using Twitter	11
Why Do You Want To Use Twitter?	11
You Are What You Tweet - Understanding the Brand Called You	11
Focus On Clarity	12
Using Twitter To Tell Your Story	13
Chapter 2	15
What are your Core values, Missions, and Promise?	15
Business Ambassador	17
Sharing Your Experiences	18
For Fun and Family	18
Collaborations	18
Community Advocacy	19
Professional Advocacy	19
Chapter 3	21
Telephone vs. Megaphone	21
The Twitter Mindset	21
Think Twitter	21
Module 2	**24**
Getting acquainted with your potential community And Learning about Twitter	**24**
Chapter 4	25

Defining Your Ideal Audience	25
Who Are You Targeting?	25
How Do I Choose The Right Audience?	26
Do You Know What Your Keywords Are?	27
How Can I Reach My Potential Audience Using Twitter?	28
Who's Following Your Fellow Industry Professionals?	30
Chapter 5	31
What Are You Really Saying?	31
What is your Twitter Tone?	31
Your Message	32
Is Your Twitter Messaging Clear?	32
Chapter 6	35
How to build your Twitter Community	35
(Your network)	35
Your Twitter Profile is the Keyhole	35
Do you have your profile optimized?	35
Content Relevancy	38
Types of Content To Post On Twitter	39
Where to Find Content to Curate	39
Types of Followers On Twitter	39
Reaching your Twitter Limits	42
Why is this even necessary?	42
What is a valid reason to have more than 5000 Twitter connections ?	43
How do you get around this small but aggravating issue?	43
Chapter 7	45
How to Engage On This Microblogging Platform	45
How to craft your tweets	45
Retweeting	46
Using Quote Retweets	46
GIFS	47
Chapter 8	48

Tweet Your Way To Thought Leadership	48
Why Should You Care About Your Online Authority	48
5 Ways To Becoming Influential Using Twitter	49
Chapter 9	50
Twitter Etiquette and Best Practices	50
Do's and Don'ts Of Twitter (More like guidelines)	50
Chapter 10	54
Twitter Chat Like A Pro	54
What Are Twitter Chats?	54
Why You Should Join Them	54
How To Participate	55
What To Do After the Twitter Chat	56
Chapter 11	58
Live-Tweeting at Events, Workshops, Conferences, and Webinars	58
Why Live Tweet	58
Volunteer vs. Duty: Community Building Technique	59
The "H" Word! (Hashtags)	60
Chapter 12	63
What are hashtags?	63
Do's and Don'ts of How To Use Hashtags to Engage	63
Finding Hashtags To Collaborate	64
Trade Show, Event, and Conference Hashtags	65
Module 3	**66**
Creating a super simple strategy	**66**
Chapter 13	67
6 Step Roadmap For Twitter Success	67
Plan for posting and sharing	71
Twitter Metrics To Track	75
Module 4	**78**
Using technology:	**78**

Twitter Tools and Resources — 78
Chapter 14 — 79
Tools Time — 79
- Twitter Search — 79
- Twitter Advanced Search — 79
- Hootsuite — 80
- TweetDeck — 81
- Tchat.io — 82
- Symplur — 82
- ManageFlitter: — 83
- Phone Apps To Download — 84

Chapter 15 — 85
Automation Is Your Virtual Assistant — 85
- Why You Need To Use It — 85
- What To Remember About Using Automation — 86

Module 5 — 87

Protect Ya Neck — 87
Chapter 16 — 88
Protecting Yourself, The consumer, and Your Business — 88
- What is Reputation Management? — 88
- How To Manage Your Online Twitter Reputation — 89
- Your Privacy Options — 89
- Protected Account (Private) — 90
- Public Account — 90
- Should You Have Two Twitter Accounts? — 91
- Key Things To Remember To Protect Your Online Twitter Reputation — 91

Chapter 17 — 93
Do you have a Twitter Policy? — 93
- Understanding Company Policy — 94
- Do Your Employees Know The Rules — 95

Final Thoughts: Twitter Marketing Unlocked　　　　　97

INTRODUCTION

Don't jump!

When it comes to Twitter you might be tempted to jump feet first and embrace the platform wholeheartedly. I do want you to embrace the platform, but jumping into Twitter without a plan is setting yourself, your brand, or business up for failure and true disappointment.

Twitter, when implemented with a sense of direction, will take you a whole lot further than randomly sending tweets, retweeting and replying whenever it feels right.

I've created this book to help provide you with direction for when you decide to use this platform to grow influence, make an impact, and increase your income. Hopefully you will walk away with strategies on how to maneuver on this platform and things I didn't know when I first joined Twitter in 2010.

Twitter will be what you make it. But, without a strategy, without purpose, without effort, you will not be able to get what you want from this network. Like Facebook, Instagram, Snapchat, and any other network you can think of, you get what you give and if you give nothing you get nothing. Twitter is no different.

Each module in this book can stand on its own. Based on where you are in your business, feel free to jump around and go back as needed. Use the questions and the exercises to help you find your path while using Twitter. Twitter is about connecting, communicating, and collaborating. As you go through this book, don't forget you may have to test and tweak along the way.

Don't be discouraged and stick with Twitter. I guarantee that if you stick with it long enough, you will see the results that you want.

MODULE 1

CREATING THE FOUNDATION

Chapter 1

Introducing your business brand and Understanding your purpose for using Twitter

Why Do You Want To Use Twitter?

Twitter IS a social network. In order for it to work for your business or organization, you have to go with the intentions of being social. It doesn't matter which platform you choose. Whether it's Twitter, Instagram, Facebook, or Pinterest, without the social aspect as a part of the strategy, nothing you do online will be successful.

As you go through the next couple chapters, I want you to think about why you want to use Twitter. The sole purpose of the next few chapters is about helping you to get clear about your purpose for this network and how Twitter can enable you to effectively connect, communicate, and collaborate with other like-minded people to grow your community.

You Are What You Tweet - Understanding the Brand Called You

You are what you tweet! Every tweet you publish is a 280 character representation of you and what you want to share with the world. Who would have guessed that one sentence can make a positive or negative impact on someone's life? I don't mean to be so dramatic, but think about how one tweet from our president can cause Twitter to go in an uproar. Just one bad tweet from a Fortune 500 brand can send its stocks tumbling down. If you don't want it to be attached to your brand, then think before you tweet it.

What do you want to be known for on Twitter? I'm not trying to scare you out of tweeting, but I don't want you to take using this social network lightly either.

Whether you are still in the process of discovering your brand or you are thinking about rebranding, start tweeting content that will be interesting to your potential audience and begin growing your presence.

Here are some questions to consider as you prepare to create your Twitter strategy.

- What is your area of expertise that you want to share with your Twitter community?
- What are your unique skills that others can appreciate?
- What subject will you be okay tweeting about all the time?

Focus On Clarity

At the end of the road of clarity, leads to the success of your business on Twitter.

How can you determine what types of content to share and discuss if you are unclear about your brand? Is your brand a clear representation that you can share with your twitterverse? Brand clarity makes it easier for you to have consistency on Twitter. If you are unclear about your brand offline, the same ambiguity will manifest itself on Twitter as well.

Do you already have a solid brand? Wonderful, keep moving to the next chapter. But if you are puzzled on how you can gain brand clarity, then continue on and take time to answer the activity questions at the end of this chapter.

Using Twitter To Tell Your Story

If you're wondering how can you share a story in 280 characters you can't. But when you string together a bunch of tweets, together they can create and develop a powerful storyline that can make an impact on its reader.

I must admit that Twitter wasn't always my favorite social network. I've had a love/hate relationship with it for several years. What I learned is that I needed to embrace what made Twitter unique. And accept its uncanny ability to connect and engage people in roughly two full sentences.

Over time, I began to realize that if I strategically develop my tweets into pieces of broken up storylines, my tweets could take my Twitter community on a journey that will make them come back daily to read more of my tweets.

Let start with some realistic questions to get you thinking about your current state of your brand.

Twitter Activity Questions:

1. Why am I in this business?
2. Why do I believe in the work I do?
3. What makes me excited about this business?
4o Do I need business (revenue) instantly?

5. Do I have time OR money to invest in my business?

6. What is my purpose for using Twitter?

7. What are my top 3-5 subject topics?

8. Why are these topics important to my community?

9. Am I ready to take on this platform and all the nuances that come with it?

Chapter 2

What are your Core values, Missions, and Promise?

When I first started using Twitter, I met many great people and had tons of interesting conversations. Although I was growing my following, I had no real brand strategy and no one knew what I did or how I could help them.

Once I realized my mistake, I had to figure out where I was and where I wanted to go using Twitter. So, I came up with 4 simple landmarks to help determine where I was on my brand journey and where I wanted to go.

To help you avoid the same mistakes I made, I want to share with you these four landmarks.

1. Is my mission and message clear to my Twitter audience?

Take a look at your Twitter bio. Does it align with what you want others to know about you and your business? Does it have too much business jargon or too little?

It's easy to get caught up worrying about what to tweet, but take a few minutes to create a Twitter bio that is unique for you. Your Twitter bio is not set in stone. Change it as many times as you need in the beginning. But, once you find one that clearly communicates your message, keep it around so it can stick for your Twitter followers.

2. Do your Tweets showcase what area of expertise you represent?

People will determine whether or not to follow you by looking at your first 1-5 tweets. Take a look at your last 5 tweets. Do they educate your Twitter community about the potential value you can offer? One way to make sure new followers get a clear idea of what kinds of content you plan on sharing is to pin a Tweet to the top of your tweets. It will stay there as long as you want it to, but changing it frequently will continue to peak the interest of your followers.

3. Do you engage and build relationships consistently?

This is the most time consuming part of the journey. Building relationships can take a few weeks or a few months. It's determined by how much you interact meaningfully on Twitter. If you're only on Twitter once every few days for only 15 minutes, your brand will take longer to stick and people will not take you seriously. I'm not saying to spend every waking hour on Twitter, but 15- 30 minutes everyday will grow your brand awareness, build valuable relationships, and create a valuable and engaging Twitter community that will amplify your brand.

4. Are you creating an Twitter experience worth sharing?

Tweeting can be boring, lonely, and quite frankly a waste of time if no one is taking the time to read what you tweeted. Your brand will not grow because no will care about who you are and the message you're trying to share. Use Twitter to deliver an effective and consistent experience that your audience will want to share, retweet, and like.

Twitter is creating features that can help with this process. Use gifs to say hello, upload a 2 minute and 20 sec video welcoming your new Twitter follower or use it to answer a questions. Livestream to your Twitter community using Periscope. Twitter even has polls that you can create. Get creative!

UNDERSTANDING WHY YOU WANT TO USE TWITTER

Everything you communicate needs to have a purpose, otherwise you are just adding to the constant stream of noise that exist in every niche. When I say noise, it's not that the content you create or share isn't any good, but there is just too much of it out there for any and everyone to consume.

What I'm about to share are some ways that Twitter can be used that you may find helpful to think about. You may want to use the platform for one of these reason or several of them. If you are unsure of your "why," it's okay. The whole purpose of talking about this now is for you to reach that level of understanding you need to understand your why.

I want to be able to share with you as many options as possible. It is not for me to tell you why you need to use Twitter. Remember everybody's business is different even if you're in the same niche or industry. Here are different ways you can consider using the social network:

Business Ambassador

When you approach Twitter as your own business ambassador, you are looking to grow your brand awareness, connect with various audiences, and hopefully generate potential leads that can lead to sales for your business. When you are focused on being your business ambassador, it is important to have a strategy in place to help guide you along this journey. In Module 3 of this book, I will share with you a simple strategy that you can implement to help you make this transition onto Twitter much easier and less time-consuming.

Sharing Your Experiences

When you choose to make Twitter about sharing your experiences, it is not necessarily about your business but more about your lifestyle and sharing the events around your life. This approach still needs a strategy. Think about the areas of your life that you would like to keep private and what you don't mind sharing with the world. Create daily themes to help keep you on track that way you still have a level of structure within the flow of things. As with anything, the main purpose is to stay consistent with the direction that you're taking if you're coming from a lifestyle approach.

For Fun and Family

Now although this book is about growing your business on Twitter by connecting, collaborating, and communicating, you may decide that you just want to be on Twitter for sharing fun content and connecting with friends and family members. Whatever route you choose to go that's fine, but remember that if you are in a professional career or are looking to grow your business online, you may want to consider making this particular profile private. In Module 5, I will discuss more about your privacy and different ways to approach your account depending on your business and personal needs.

Collaborations

Collaborations are a necessity to your business! In my humble opinion, I believe LinkedIn and Twitter are the best platforms for forging great collaborations with others in your niche and outside of it. I always refer to Twitter as the lowest hanging fruit. The barrier to connecting with people is lower on Twitter than connecting on LinkedIn. Consider using this platform as a gateway to connect on other platforms you might be on. I know Facebook tends to be the go-to platform for forging relationships, but it may be time to rethink that strategy and consider using Twitter as a way to grow your collaborative network.

Community Advocacy

Are you a not for profit organization or a community-based business? Twitter should be your go-to platform to share your purpose and your passion with a community of like-minded people that you have found through hashtags, tweets, and outreach. There is no better way to make a powerful impact than to share what's important to the lives of the people you are hoping to connect with. This social network has a huge potential for spreading the word quickly and for going viral. When you are choosing to be a community advocate, having a little finesse goes a long way and having a strategy in place will be what you need to ensure your organization's long-term success.

Professional Advocacy

Last but not least, Twitter can be used as an advocate for your professional career or industry. What I mean by this is, for example, you are a nutritionist, you may decide to use Twitter as a way to connect with other nutritionists, share industry news, and catch up on certain industry events that are happening within your profession. Depending on what industry you are in, you may find you have more people using Twitter as a way of educating and staying on top of what's happening in their industry. People who only tweet or lurk for industry news tends to fall off the bandwagon of tweeting and only come on the platform when they are needing something. Don't be that person who disappears for long stretches of time. Try to continue being active on the network so that your profile doesn't appear to be a ghost town when you are not tweeting out industry information. If you disappear, so will your tweets and the people who follow you probably not see your tweets when you do begin tweeting. You may be wondering how to keep your Twitter feed active when you don't have the time. My best advice is to consider adding a little automation to the process. I will touch on this a little bit later in the chapter about automation.

Twitter Activity Question:

1. How do you want to use Twitter? (start a new relationship, nurture existing relationships, or improve relationships)

2. Is my mission and message clear to my Twitter audience?

3. Do your tweets showcase what area of expertise you represent?

4. Do you engage and build relationships consistently?

5. Are you creating a Twitter experience worth sharing?

6. Why are you wanting to use Twitter?

Chapter 3

Telephone vs. Megaphone

The Twitter Mindset

Before you can begin to master Twitter, you have to have the right mindset approaching the network. This 280 character platform culture is not the same as Facebook, Instagram, or even Snapchat.

Twitter is the laid back, a bit more fun companion to LinkedIn. This microblogging platform is where gifs, emojis, and bitmojis are all accepted when saying hello for the first time. An introduction doesn't have to be a formal sounding ending with a period instead of an exclamation mark.

The clients that I have worked with tend to stay away from Twitter because they are unsure how to merge their current brand with the culture of the network. My advice to them is treat Twitter like you would handle any networking event. Go with the intentions of meeting key people but be open to engaging with random people who are showing up. You never know if that new acquaintance could turn into a major key player for your business.

Keep an open mind when networking on Twitter!

Think Twitter

Don't join the network blaring about your new project, service, app, or business especially if you haven't taken time to connect with people.

No one will listen, more importantly, no one cares and that is the quickest way to get blocked or muted.

How do we use our cell phones when making a call? It's usually one to one conversation, and on occasion, it may be a group call. That is how I want you to think about this network. Think of your interaction as a phone call with occasional group calls involving potential friends.

Are you unsure if you're a megaphone on Twitter? Take a look at your Twitter news stream. What does it look like? Is there anyone engaging with you? Have you given or received any new likes (favorites)? How many times have you tweeted the exact same tweet within the last week? Be honest with yourself. What do you see?

You may be new to Twitter or you've finally decided to put forth the effort into making the social network work for you. I want you to remember this formula.

The Right Twitter Mindset + Interaction + Listening = Twitter Success

Don't be afraid to reach out to new people. Twitter is not rigid like other platforms. This network is considered the place you go to when you want to meet new people locally and across the world. All conversations are potential ones you can join unless it has been shared as a private DM.

Twitter Activity Questions:

1. How do you feel about the network?
2. Take a brief look at your account: Does it look like your making telephone call or using a megaphone?

3. What would you like to happen by using Twitter?

Module 2

Getting acquainted with your potential community And Learning about Twitter

Chapter 4

Defining Your Ideal Audience

Each platform is special and appeals to different people for a certain set of reason. Twitter is no different. It appeals to a variety of people the different reasons. Some like the platform for its brevity and others can appreciate the amount of conversation and engagement that they get from being on the platform. I want you to take a moment and think of it like this, you act somewhat different if you're attending a professional conference versus just a general mixer or family engagement. It's not that you're a different person, you act accordingly to the environment that you take part in. These same principles apply when you are choosing a network like Twitter.

It doesn't matter how clear your message is or what kinds of emotions you can evoke if you're talking to the wrong people. You need to be able to create content that is :

1. Appropriate for Twitter
2. Engaging and enjoyable for your audience
3. SEO friendly for Google

When you know who you are trying to communicate with, it is easier to share challenges and problems that your audience may be having. You will communicate in a way that's relatable and develop a community quicker that is interested in your brand or your business.

Who Are You Targeting?

Before we take a deep dive into your Twitter strategy, let's start by going over who will be your target audience on Twitter. Knowing your target audience WILL change as you begin to work with certain groups and your understanding of them evolves.

Don't get flustered if you don't know yet, pick the best group for right now. Your target audience is NOT set in stone. Go beyond thinking only about your audience demographics. Think about where they work, industry titles, psycho-demographic, hobbies, and interests. You are multifaceted and so is your potential audience.

Your target audience is NOT everyone, even if your products, service, or app can be beneficial for everyone. Start with one person, one group, and one topic in mind so that you are able to focus and take action with connecting, marketing, and selling to an audience who wants what you have to offer to them.

How Do I Choose The Right Audience?

Depending on who you ask, this could almost be considered a trick question. If you are a newbie to building a business, starting an organization or creating your own brand without a target audience, start with thinking about who would you like to work with. Who makes the most sense for your business? Let's go one step further. Who would you like to work with that can afford to pay you? Not everyone you want to work for will be able to pay your fees and that is fine.

I know people don't like to talk about money because they believe that it's all about serving others. But a business that is not making money truly isn't a business. When you think of the audience, keep in mind who you are providing a service to may not be the audience who pays you (think B2B). In this case, you would have 2 different target audiences for Twitter.

There are several questions you should ask yourself that can help you identify your right audience in case you need the extra help. But, if you are familiar with your target audience, feel free to skip to the next chapter.

Ask Yourself :

- Who have you worked for in the past that you wouldn't mind continue working for?
- Am I ready to work with B2B clients or larger organizations?
- Who has the customer base for your ideal target audience?
- What type of people do you work with and interact with the best?
- Do you have an ideal location for your best clients? (This is especially important if you are a local business!)
- What are the specific challenges you can solve for your potential clients?

Spend time answering these questions. After you have found a target audience to start, you are ready to begin connecting on Twitter.

Do You Know What Your Keywords Are?

What are "keywords?" These are specific words that you want to be synonymous with your brand, business, organization, your product or service. These key terms should be related to your expertise. For example, Ashley Hill, the CEO of College Prep Ready, is a Scholarship Search Strategist. Can you guess her main keywords? Scholarships, #Collegechat, and #scholarshipchat. If you type those words into the Twitter search bar, her name will appear.

It may be tempting to formalize a long list of key terms like you would do for your website or blog, but that is not necessary for Twitter. Limit your keywords to just a handful. For instance, my top three keywords are Twitter marketing, social media, and branding. I have a couple more that I will use interchangeable, but those are my main keywords.

How Can I Reach My Potential Audience Using Twitter?

Twitter.com is an underutilized databased with a wealth of information that goes under the radar. You can find information about companies, their business interests, a company's target audience and some of their marketing activities like what conferences they attend. Most of it is public information that you can use for creating a comprehensive database of potential prospects.

Are you still wondering exactly what kinds of information you can potentially obtain from searching on Twitter? I've provided you with a list below:

- Residence (state and sometimes the city)
- School enrolled or attended
- Website
- Phone number (depending on the industry)
- Volunteer activities
- Hobbies
- Family members
- Employer
- Board memberships (for-profit and nonprofit)
- Favorite travel destinations
- Pet lover
- Undeniable weaknesses
- General age base on certain information that is being tweeted

Stop reading for one second and attempt to look up some of this information for yourself on Twitter? What can you find out? Did you believe this was possible?

Pro Search Tips:

- Try adding parentheses around your keyword in the search bar. It's similar to searching on Google. Twitter will find that particular word together if you are using phrases.
- Add a question mark after the word or phrase if you're looking for questions about the keyword.

- Search using a particular hashtag.
- Use partial words or abbreviations someone industries use them instead of the entire word as a character saving technique.
- If you are trying to find tweets with a certain sentiment, try adding a happy face, sad face, or angry face emoji in addition to the keyword(s).

Who's Following Your Fellow Industry Professionals?

Still having a difficult time trying to connect with your potential community? Look towards your industry competitors. Who are they following and who is following them? There is always some organization that has been on Twitter longer and have already built up their online Twitter community. Don't feel bad for trying to connect with their followers.

People have a choice. They can connect with you or stick to being a loyal follower of that competitor. The same goes for connecting with people who follow a certain trade publication or informational source for your industry and target audience. Don't recreate the wheel and start from scratch when you don't have to. Make a list and rotate your engagement methods until you have built up your own relationships and community on Twitter.

Chapter 5

What Are You Really Saying?

In this section, we will discuss your tone, your message, where and how you should tell your story. Show your personality! You don't have to be a comedian to be relatable. You just have to be yourself. When you're taking the time to create relatable content, the parts of you that make you unique is what people will see.

What is your Twitter Tone?

In essence, your Twitter tone is your part of your brand's online personality. It is the human element that you want to convey to someone who is reading and engaging with your tweets. A personal brand personality can be relatively easy to portray on the platform more than a company or an organization brand. The organization tone on Twitter should align with the mission, values, and culture of the organization.

Twitter Activity Exercise:

- ❖ Combining your brand's voice and your vision, think about the content you want to share. Write down 5 content ideas that should relate to the kinds of followers you want to attract.

Your Message

The quickest way to make people run from your business is to confuse them. Your brand message should align with the identity you want to be known for. This is especially important in the beginning stages of presenting yourself on Twitter or any major network online or offline. Nail down the message you want to communicate and stick to it. I will say the hardest thing about your message is not the fact that you will probably rebrand at some point in time. But it's sticking to the message once you have it and you see that it is relating to your audience. The urge to change and doubt your message value will set in. Don't listen to your feelings and rely on your brain. Know that 8 times out of 10, your message is connecting to your audience of choice. So stick to it once you see that it is working, And in this case, resist the urge to change your message.

Is Your Twitter Messaging Clear?

A clear brand message can captivate your potential community and draw them in and have them continuously looking out for your tweets in their timeline.

How do you know if your messaging is clear? You will attract potential business connections that are looking for collaborations and speaking engagements on the topics you mention on Twitter. You will be seen as an authority figure within your industry. When was the last time someone wanted to connect with you because of something you've shared on Twitter? If it hasn't' been recent, there might be a problem with your messaging and it could use some tweaking.

When your message resonates with your true audience, Twitter truly becomes your "word of mouth" marketing tool. People will share tweets with others letting them know to look out and connect with you. Twitter becomes the bridge that allows you to be separated by only 3 degrees from the rest of the world.

Here are 3 main things to remember about your brand message on Twitter:

1. Clarity is your key to success. The clearer you are about your brand, your offerings, and your audience, the easier it will be to create tweets that attracts your Twitter tribe.

2. There is power in having consistency. You have to be relentless in showing up on Twitter. It doesn't matter if you fall off. Get back on and keep going. Life happens, but you can't keep rebranding every time you fall off and come back. It will confuse your community.

3. Keep connecting, grow your connections, build and develop relationships. Twitter can be considered a platform used to share content on a one to many level, but it is the most powerful when its used for connecting one to one.

Twitter Activity Questions:

1. How do you want them to feel?

2. What message are you trying to communicate?

3. What emotion is your brand supposed to evoke in your potential clients?

4. What motivates them?

5.. What do you want your customers to do after they hear your message?

6. What action do you want them to take? (CTA)

7. How will you lead them into the sales funnel?

Chapter 6

How to build your Twitter Community (Your network)

Your Twitter Profile is the Keyhole

Your Twitter profile is the first thing people will look at when they have decided to follow you on Twitter. It is the keyhole that they see before they insert the key and choose to begin the journey of connecting with you. The foundation for building a great community on Twitter starts with a great Twitter profile.

Let me preface by saying there is no one profile that will attract all of your potential audience. As with everything else, it's about trial and error. You have to know what your objectives are and then you can create a bio, a call to action (CTA) and a place for people to visit.

Do you have your profile optimized?

Profile optimization is about making sure your profile is up-to-date. That means you have taken the time to upload a recent image of yourself, not just any picture, but a picture that people will use to recognize you when they meet you in person.

You only have 160 characters to make an impression. Fill out your bio. Use your best judgment and remember this is what people will see first when they are choosing to connect with you.

- How do you want to position yourself to your Twitter

community?
- Do you want to be a resource for others?

- Are you mainly using the network to connect with others?

These are just a few things to consider as you are filling out your Twitter profile. Don't get bogged down with making it perfect because over time I'm sure you will adjustments accordingly.

Is your goal to increase traffic to your website? If so, having a link that goes to your website is ideal. If your goal is to share insights on a subject you are passionate about, your Twitter link should lead to that source. Whatever it is that you want people to know more about this will determine how your profile will be created and what key terms should be added.

For example, if you are an acupuncturist, then you will want to share the types of services you have in the office and whether you specialize in specific ailments like back pain, fibromyalgia, or neuropathy, etc. You can share office hours, office email, or a front office phone number for people to reach out to you. Do you see how by adding those few keywords along with the fact that you're an acupuncturist can help attract people with a problem who are looking for someone of your specialty profession?

Profile Tips Consider

➢ Remove a blurry profile picture or extremely old or inconspicuous image

➢ Change up your links, in your profile. It doesn't always have to be a link to the blog. Send them to sales pages, a podcast, or to another social platform.

- Do you have a memorable Twitter handle? One that makes you look human and not similar to a spambot.

- Creative titles only you understand. Provide benefits of over fancy title. (For ex. Guru, Ninja, hacks, or Mogul)

- Limit your use of hashtags because they are not really necessary. Hashtags and keywords are one in the same when it comes to your Twitter bio.

- Use a logo if it appropriate. It is okay to use pictures of you and your business location. (Local business tip)

- Create a branded Twitter header. Use it to tell people what you do, upcoming events, or achievements and show some personality. Nothing obscene Use a tagline that can double as something memorable.

- Have you optimized for keywords? Don't overstuff your profile and keep it simple.

Twitter Pro Tip:

Use a notepad or a tool like Evernote to write down between 3 to 5 different Twitter profile bios. The trick is to master a way to make an impact with 160 characters and it will take creating a few different bios. Make life easier for you by keeping them all in one location. Once you've created these bios, alternate every two to four weeks and see if that particular bio attracts your ideal audience.

If you notice that the wrong people are following you, there is nothing wrong with changing your bio to one of your alternate bios. Or, if you notice the bio you have is attracting the right audience, then create two or three more bios with similar words that you can alter after a period of time.

Content Relevancy

Content is essential to growing a following on Twitter and engaging the right social tribe. In essence, your content has to be relevant to your target audience . The message you share can be insightful and make an impact on someone needing to hear it. But if you're sharing it with the wrong audience, it will fall on deaf ears.

When you're creating content to create brand awareness, ask yourself these questions:

- What questions do your potential clients have?
- Does your content speak to their issues in the words that your potential clients use?
- How will your content influence your relationship with them?
- How will you measure the ROI/ Impact/ Transformation of the content that you've created?
- What kinds of information do they need?
- Why do they need the information?
- Where do they seek the information?
- What content do they NEED to make their lives easier?
- What support do they need?
- What content can they help you to create?

Types of Content To Post On Twitter

- Links to your articles - Drive people into your website
- Live video
- Native video uploaded
- Images (Static or gifs) - Use your images to give a call to action
- Promotional Content (Webinars, events)
- Interactive questions (FAQ, Open-Ended, Fill in the blanks, Conversational)
- Contest
- Challenges (free or low cost)
- Giveaways

Where to Find Content to Curate

The World Wide Web is just that, a worldwide place of content that seems to be a never-ending stream of information. It is not so much where to find content, but how to make it easier to curate content that is suitable for your audience. Since this book is all about Twitter, I would stay start by finding relevant sources of content you want to share with your audience. A content source can include other tweeters in the industry, associations, parallel industries, or people who share content your audience will enjoy reading.

Types of Followers On Twitter

Not all followers on Twitter are created equal. It helps to understand this when socializing on the network. I do believe every Twitter follower has a purpose and can help you grow your following in some way. I want to share with you the 5 main followers that you may come across while you are connecting on Twitter. The reason I'm giving you this information is not so that you can avoid people, but so you can understand the type of community that exists in this space.

The Professional Lurker

The lurker is just that, they lurk, they read, and they will even share your tweets in DM and private messages. They will share your content in emails to themselves or to other people, but you will never know that they exist.

So why are they important?

They are important because they help spread the word about you, your purpose, and business. They share educational content that you've produced and put you in front of new audiences. It's a mutually beneficial relationship you didn't know existed. Remember this the next time you say to yourself that no one is engaging. Think about all the potential lurkers who might be learning from you.

The Retweeter

These type of people are also great for spreading the word and giving your content traction which increases your impressions and reach. They may never buy from you, or even read your content….. ever ! But, they will share and that is absolutely fine because you need all the eyes you can get to the content you've worked so hard to produced or curate. Don't get mad when all they do is retweet, but rejoice at the thought of it.

The Conversationalist

The conversationalist gives you wings! They are similar to the retweeter, but they don't retweet your content. Instead, they will respond to every tweet you put out there. They are the engagers who give you a reason to come back to Twitter just to have a conversation over something you've shared. Conversationalists bring life to anyone's Twitter stream and will create an enjoyable environment. Remember these people will probably never purchase from you, read your blogs, or retweet your content and you need to be okay with that. Twitter, after all, is a social network and you are there to be social. Keep the conversations going.

The Collaborator

These people on Twitter are looking for mutual relationships. The collaborators prefer to do a retweet for a retweet or a share for a share. Collaborators are usually looking for ways to grow their community and to get in front of your audience preferably which is not a bad thing. The key to making this work is to make sure that the agreement is mutually beneficial. A one-sided agreement can result in you or the other party walking away unhappy and feeling used. You will feel discouraged from being active on Twitter. Even though it's just Twitter, do not take this type of relationship lightly because it may work out and you will be surprised by all the potential opportunities that can flourish. But, if it goes sour, it can make for really intense situations.

The Silent Lead

The silent lead, this is the lead you don't see coming. They don't retweet, engage in conversations with you, or talk about you to other people. The silent leads start off as lurkers. They're watching, reading, and consuming your content all without you ever knowing it. This is why your Twitter brand needs to be on point. Then, one day they're on your email list. The next day they've purchased your book or may even schedule a consultation call. Statistics show that said over half of the people on Twitter never tweet, period. If leads are your main reason for being on the network, it will be in your best interest to keep your Twitter account active and provide consistent value.

Reaching your Twitter Limits

Have you reached your 5,000 Twitter following limit? And now, are you unable to follow any more of your target community? To continue growing your followers, you 'll want to consider removing your inactive, fake, and unfollowers so that you can continue connecting successfully on Twitter.

Why is this even necessary?

Twitter has a stupid rule that once you reach 5,000 Twitter community members, you can not add more than about 10% of your current following. (Remember all numbers are relative and slightly differ per account)

According to Twitter's policy, (which you can read here: https://support.twitter.com/articles/68916), it's done to limit abuse of the platform and adding thousands of people just to have a large account.

The sad truth is we really don't authentically connect with that many people on Twitter and we don't NEED more than 5000. But, having the option to connect with more people is an option that is needed based on your determined marketing objective.

What is a valid reason to have more than 5000 Twitter connections ?

The number of people you're connected with on Twitter can be a valuable asset to your business and personal brand for market research or bringing in new customers for example.

Hey, who doesn't want a bigger Twitter community?!

But, whatever your reason is for wanting more followers, having the option to do so is what we all want on any network.

How do you get around this small but aggravating issue?

Let me start by saying, congratulations on reaching your 5,000 Twitter following limit!

I'm happy you hung in there on Twitter to achieve that goal. But, what can you do about the hold on your account? You can wait until you have more people following you. If you're impatient like me, this probably isn't the best option for you. But, if you are not in any rush, you have a few more options. Keep tweeting, keep engaging and being helpful to others, and you will find that people will add you to their community.

Additionally, you can begin the process of manually unfollowing accounts. You can go to twitter.com/yourprofile and start removing people you haven't connected with, those that haven't bother to follow you back, and followers who have given up on Twitter. It's another time-consuming option, but faster than the first option and it will free up your account so you can continue growing your Twitter community.

Use a tool to unfollow accounts. There are quite a few tools that you can use that have a free and paid version to help with making the process quicker and less time-consuming. One tool I recommend is ManageFlitter. It has a freemium which allows you to remove 100 people every 24 hours and there is a paid option that allows you to remove the upper limits allowed by Twitter. If you don't have time, then consider using any number of tools that are suitable for your needs.

Growing your Twitter account shouldn't be a hassle! Take control of your account so that you can connect with anyone AND everyone that you want to.

Chapter 7

How to Engage On This Microblogging Platform

Twitter is not like Facebook where you can write an entire story in a single tweet. It's not like Instagram, Snapchat, or Pinterest where an image can tell a thousand words. Twitter is about how you can express a clear and concise thought that can make an instant connection with someone. Although, I do advise you to add images to your tweets when you possible, it's not necessary. Twitter at its core is all about being social. It an extension of your social life, a place where you can develop and grow authentic personal and business relationships with people around the world.

The more social you are on Twitter, your ROI increases especially if your investment is time. Engagement starts with a simple tweet. Be active! Although this seems fairly simple, it can be difficult to do. Active tweeters are the most engaging. So, tweet consistently and always provide value. I like to tell my clients to not wait to start engaging on Twitter when you need a community. The time to start building is now.

How to craft your tweets

Crafting a tweet is not rocket science and soon you will become a pro at it with enough practice. Since Twitter has increased their character limit from 140 to 280 characters, people have increasingly become more creative on how to craft the "perfect tweet." There is no such thing as a perfect tweet technically. A perfect tweet for all purposes is one that gets the type of engagement you were wanting to achieve your goal. How you choose to format your tweets is completely up to you and your organization. You're only limited by your own creativity. Get ideas on the type of tweets that your audience engages with by taking a peep at similar industries. But, don't be afraid to think outside the box and look at industries completely opposite for true creativity. On Twitter, I'm always looking for different ways to say the same thing.

Retweeting

Retweeting is an underused feature of the network. Most people nowadays opt to favorite a tweet instead of sharing a tweet. Show someone that you care and their content is worth sharing with others. There is no better way to begin engaging with your community than to show them that you value their content too. Retweet someone you admire today and often.

Using Quote Retweets

A quote retweet is a retweet with a comment attached to the original tweet. I find this to be exceptionally helpful for keeping the conversation going and allowing people to see exactly what you are commenting on. This kind of tweet is also helpful during twitter chats and offers people different ways to be part of the conversation. Also, this extends the reach of that particular tweet. Here is an example of a quote tweet with a good friend of mine, Liz Evangelatos of @Askforliz, who is a social media consultant who provides support for real estate agents.

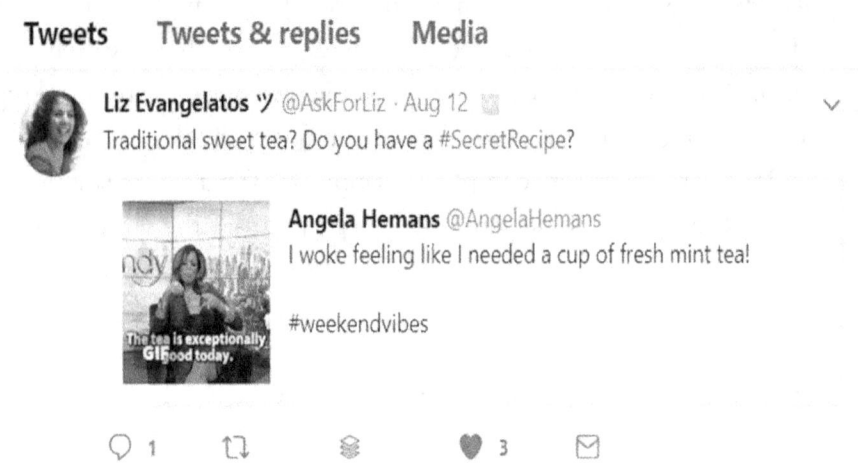

GIFS

Who doesn't like a good gif? It can make you smile, laugh, feel sad, or get angry. Gifs which stands for Graphics Interchange Format is one of the best ways to add context to a tweet. If you're sarcastic like I am, sarcasm can be difficult to express on Twitter. Therefore I use gifs and recommend others use them liberally when tweeting. As with anything, there is a time and place for action appropriate gifs. Pay attention to what is being done and the words on this 3 sec loop. Don't get blocked for using content for mature audiences in a PG-13 conversation.

Chapter 8

Tweet Your Way To Thought Leadership

Have you been working towards becoming a thought leader within your specific industry? Now, are you ready to take it to the next level and wonder how Twitter can play a role in building your expertise? Maybe you've been wondering if this is a path you should take, but not sure how to start the process with Twitter. I can tell you that this social network can help grow your authority within your industry if you are willing to do the work.

A thought leader can inspire and create a direct impact with their influence. Whether you are a writer, executive, entrepreneur, consultant, physician, or an educator, anyone can become a thought leader with work and determination to achieve greater.

Why Should You Care About Your Online Authority

How would it feel to be the go-to person in your industry and people automatically trust you because of your knowledge? Building authority can ultimately lead to increased impact, influence and income. As your credibility grows within an industry, it will create opportunities for more strategic partnerships, referral relationships, and speaking opportunities.

Thought leadership provides you with the ability to create a lasting impact on a topic that you're passionate about. Using Twitter to build your thought leadership can unlock a whole new level of possibilities you never thought was possible. Your ability to establish thought leadership will spark even more online and offline business for you.

5 Ways To Becoming Influential Using Twitter

1. Know what you want to be an authority in. If you're a writer ,but you focus on healthcare, own it. Or, if you are a business consultant for women executives, the key is to stick to your expertise.

2. Share tweets about your industry's trends, your own evergreen content or opinion content consistently on your timeline.

3. Be a credible source by exposing yourself to new audiences through webinars, telesummits, live video and a contributing guest blogger. Share everything with your community.

4. Participate in Twitter chats that showcase your expertise in addition to finding chats where you can be a guest participant.

5. Build social proof. Social proof on Twitter can begin to develop through the relationships you have with other influencers in the industry. Share positive reviews and testimonials you have received from industry professionals and from your Twitter community.

As your circle of influence grows on Twitter, your personal and business network, community supporters, and allies will directly expand in response to it all. The journey to become a thought leader is not an easy road to travel especially if you're starting out on Twitter. But, if you choose to accept the challenge, it will be well worth the effort and could be the next important step in taking you to the next level within your profession.

Chapter 9

Twitter Etiquette and Best Practices

You can't acknowledge mistakes that you didn't realize you made in the first place. But, once you've made them and it's been brought to your attention, you need to acknowledge it, apologize, and do your best to correct it.

Mistakes are going to happen. Mistakes when tweeting will happen, but it's not the end of the world, at least for most people.

Do's and Don'ts Of Twitter (More like guidelines)

1. Do Put Interesting People On Twitter List

In Chapter 9, I talk about what Twitter list is and how they can save you time on the network. Every time you log into the network and you come across someone interesting who could be a referral partner, a mentor, collaborator, or a friend, that person should go on a list. Your time is precious, and if you're busy like me, you don't have 30 minutes to spend looking for someone continue the conversation with on Twitter. When you only have 5- 10 minutes to spare for Twitter, the goal is to make every minute count.

2. Don't Tweet Only Negative Tweets

You can choose to be a negative Nelly, but you have to decide if is that really what you want people to remember you for. Do you want to be *THAT* Twitter account? There will always be something negative happening in every industry. This should not be the only information that you can share on Twitter. Mix it up, a little negative, a little positive, and a little indifferent content on Twitter. Now, if this IS part of your brand, then do what you believe will work best to grow your brand and increase your visibility.

3. Do Retweet Others

Who doesn't like to be noticed? Most people wouldn't mind a little appreciation for the content that they share on Twitter. It feels good to know that someone values what you share and that it has helped them in some way. Be that person who makes an impact by retweeting others. If you need more convincing about why you should retweet others, ask yourself this question. Would I like someone to share my tweets? If you answered no, then don't retweet it, but if you answered "yes", then do unto others as you would like done to you!

4. Don't Use Direct Messages (DMs) To Spam People

If you send people a direct message (DM) on Twitter that contains a link before you have even talked to them, you are guilty of sending spam to that person. Asking people to take part in activities without first offering to help can also be considered spam. Are you sending the same message multiple times to people by DM? This is also spam. Spam can get you banned, especially in a country like Canada. If too many people complain about you for participating in spam-like activities, your Twitter account can be temporarily blocked or completely removed.

5. Do Update Your Profile Image

Do you look drastically different from your profile image on Twitter? Is your image a decade old? Have you recently rebranded and changed colors on your profile image (logo) if you are a personal brand? If you have said yes or even maybe, then it is time to update your profile and reacquaint yourself to your Twitter community. Your profile image is the first point of contact with a stranger. Do you want them to believe you are a spambot, or an inactive tweeter? Use this opportunity to put your best self out there.

6. Do Tweet And Provide Value

You now have 280 character plus gifs, pictures, and video to provide value on Twitter. Don't let it go to waste! Use tweets to provide helpful information, insights, news updates, trends, and to make someone smile. Space is the limit. Don't waste your time and other people's time just tweeting about what you have eaten for breakfast, lunch, and dinner unless you are a fitness instructor. Personal updates are fine just as long they are not the only updates you do every day. I share occasional updates of what I am eating or drinking because it makes me relatable and down to earth. Diversity is the spice of life and I don't want people thinking I'm a robot and neither should you.

7. Don't Tag Strangers In Tweets

How rude! You wouldn't ask someone to be a reference for a job that doesn't know you. So why would you tag complete strangers on a tweet that is unfamiliar to you? That is not the best way to get your tweets seen and make new friends. In fact, that would be the perfect way to get blocked or muted on Twitter. *Don't be that person!*

8. Do Save Twitter Searches And Hashtags

This is another time-saving hack for Twitter. Save your commonly search items (CSI) on Twitter. If you are looking for business leads, referral partners, Twitter chats, or keywords, then this is the way to go. Use this feature so you don't have to spend time fighting with autocorrect on your phone or desktop. Take a look at the example below to see how you can save your CSI.

First, type the keyword in the search box and click search. Click the 3 dots that you see and it will give you the option for search settings and below that "save this search." Click save. Anytime you partially type the word, it will appear for you to click and continue searching on Twitter.

Chapter 10

Twitter Chat Like A Pro

Twitter chats are still one of the most undervalued and underused activities on Twitter. Spending 30 minutes in a chat is the easiest way to be part of the conversation and attract followers who are interested in the same topic. You can attend chats in your industry, your personal interest or chats that attract your target audience. After the chat is over, now is the best time continue the conversation. You can follow up with that person on Twitter just like you would when attending in-person events.

What Are Twitter Chats?

Twitter chats are what Facebook groups are to Facebook or what LinkedIn groups are to LinkedIn. Twitter chats are the groups of Twitter. It is where people come together to tweet about a specific topic using a specific hashtag. Twitter chats is one of the best aspects of Twitter and provide the phenomenal opportunity for networking. It's a shame that more people do not participate in them. Hopefully, with more awareness, this will change.

Why You Should Join Them

Are you looking to grow your Twitter following? Do you want to increase your business visibility? Would you like to build influence and make an impact on Twitter? If you said yes to any of them, then you should consider joining Twitter chats and scheduling them into your week's activities. Participating on Twitter chats can help you do all that I mention above and more. Twitter is the lowest hanging fruit of all of the social media platforms. It is the simplest platform to connect with complete strangers and create some type of mutual bond. You can bond with others over topics that are important to you whether it's personal and or business-related. Twitter chats give you an opportunity to connect with people in various industries in which you wouldn't normally have access to connect with them . If you're looking to drive traffic to your website there is no better way to do it than to join in conversations that are already taking place on the network. The main complaints I hear from my clients is "how to engage" and "how to approach the conversations with strangers?" I tell them Twitter chats are the answer to their problems. The conversation are already taking place. You only have to join them.

How To Participate

Hashtags are your key to participating in Twitter chats. They are used to make the conversations cohesive and easy to follow for participants . These chats are usually started off by talking about whatever the topic is at the time. Some chats have a host and guests and others just have a host and the community answers. Questions asked are either showing with Q1, Q2, Q3 or T1, T2, T3, (Q stands for question and T stands for topic). When someone answers, most time it good etiquette to add A1, A2, A3, A4 so others know what questions or topics you are answering in the Twitter chat.

Conversations can sometimes go off topic! Don't shy away from engaging in off topic conversations. They can be the most enjoyable and entertaining part of the Twitter chat. General conversation that take place have nothing to do with the topic that is being discussed are where many friendships are forged. In most cases, these types of discussions are welcome because it helps to build and nurture relationships and grow the chat's visibility.

In the example below you can follow a Twitter chat that has taken place.

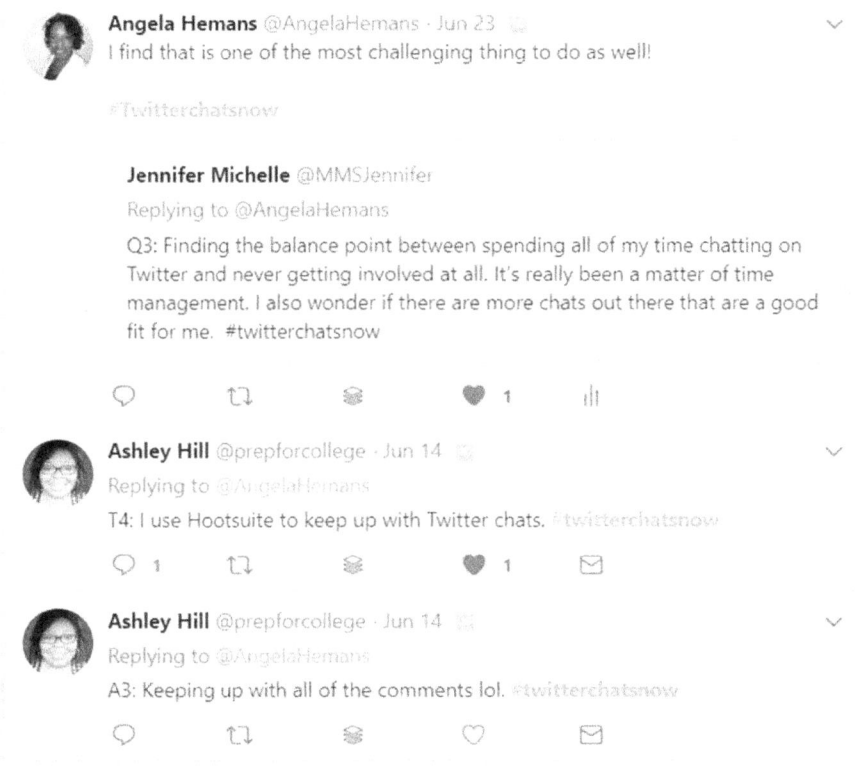

What To Do After the Twitter Chat

You just spent the last 30 minutes to an hour participating in a wonderful conversation with people that you just met on Twitter. What are you supposed to do now? Your next steps after the chat maybe one of the most important steps after participating on the Twitter chat. Take 5 to 10 minutes after you have participated in the chat to complete the following 3 steps:

1. Follow everyone that participated in the chat, retweeted your tweets, or liked any of your tweets during the chat. When you do this, not only does it show you are interested in the people, but it can also help grow your following a lot faster than just adding random people. These people are more likely to follow you back because they are familiar with the chat you just participated in together. You are no longer just a stranger and you have created the first touch point to someone who was unfamiliar with you and your business.

2. Add the people you just connected with to a Twitter list. You don't want to lose track of the people you just spent an hour talking to online. It doesn't matter if there is two people or a hundred people, add them to a private or public list that is titled by the name of the chat. You would want to do this so that if you don't have time to participate in future cats you can always take a few minutes and connect with them just to say hello.

3. Don't be afraid to take any conversations to direct messages (DMs). If you see an opportunity to continue the discussion further privately, do so. I have personally grown and nurture my own personal and professional network by taking some conversation offline, either by direct message, Skype, or Zoom. In some cases, I'll even share my phone number so we can start off texting. Feel the conversation out, don't be too quick to pitch someone, and that will be the last DM you share with that person.

Chapter 11

Live-Tweeting at Events, Workshops, Conferences, and Webinars

These type of tweets are popular for events, conference, in-person meetings, live webinars, or tele-summits. Creating a hashtag for the event and having the attendees use it to tweet will bring about awareness of the event and can spark the interest of potential future attendees.

Why Live Tweet

Social media including Twitter is all about connecting with others. Live tweeting not only allows you to connect with those at the conference, but people who would like to go to the conference that can not attend. It offers the ability to feel like you are still part of the event with the attendees.

Live tweeting when properly implemented can be used to make an positive impact on the conference culture. Use this live aspect to increase the awareness for each of the conference speakers and to share out their message. If you are an event professional or creator, live-tweeting can be viewed as an added bonus for your speakers, more visibility that is not limited to just in-person attendees.

Are you looking for way to increase your conference attendees and pack out your event? Would you like an effective way to find relevant speakers for the upcoming event? There is no better way to organically spread the word about your event than "Word of Tweet" in 280 characters. Who needs Twitter ads when you can have ambassadors of events as tweeters?

Volunteer vs. Duty: Community Building Technique

The worst thing you can do is to force someone who isn't comfortable tweeting to help live-tweet during the event. Instead, find willing volunteers to be active participants in this event activity. If there are a few tweeters who can help increase the effect, think about giving away a few free conference tickets in exchange for their participation. Do you have an expandable conference budget? Try hiring out these duties to a marketing company or freelance consultants. With everything going on with planning, preparing, and execution of your event, you don't need this additional burden Contract it out.

Once you have your group of tweeter volunteers, make them feel appreciated and include them in a pre-conference meet-up. Take some time to organize a pre-conference workshop to help the newer tweeters who have volunteered and need some extra guidance. Make sure everyone knows what workshops or keynote they will be attending so all of the tweeters won't be in the same room at the same time. To help make the process run smoother, provide electrical outlets to your team (if available) and when possible share the speaker's notes of quotables with them.

The purpose of live-tweeting is share as much about the event on that platform without boring your Twitter community.

The "H" Word! (Hashtags)

Hashtags will be the bond that unites your paying attendees whether virtual or in-person event. It will also be the connector for the ones that were in limbo about attending the event, but wasn't convinced of the value it could bring to them.

Your conference hashtag needs to be an extension of your conference title.

Here are 3 things to consider when creating an event hashtag:

1. Make it easy to remember.

2. Spelling should be as simple as possible. Keep in mind that you still only have 280 characters. Although that is an increase from the original 140 characters, you want people to have as much space to write out their full thoughts.

3. Attach the year on the hashtag. If it's an annual event this is the best way to keep track of previous, current and future years of Twitter content.

Now that you've taken time to create this hashtag, how do you go about making sure everyone knows about it? Put it everywhere, on everything, and by telling everyone at least 3 times. (Well maybe not 3 times, but at least twice!)

If you are not quite sure what I mean by everything, I'll share the following list of places you can add your hashtags.

- On Twitter accounts and tweets sent
- Website page
- Conference sales page
- Email opt-in
- All social media accounts content (Instagram, Facebook, snapchat, DM (when appropriate), Quora, Pinterest, Periscope, Live Video, LinkedIn, social and professional groups, Google Plus, and Tumblr. (Any other networks you might be on)
- Social media banners
- Any social media geofilters
- Emails sent
- Email Signature
- Snail mail
- Marketing materials
- T-shirts
- Conference name tags
- Conference Swag bags
- Hotel Key knobs
- Post-conference content
- Post-conference emails

Feel free to let me know any other creatives ways you've shared a hashtag that I didn't mention in the list. Be liberal with where you choose to share your event hashtag. The more people that know about your event is a better chance of increasing the event's visibility and awareness for upcoming events.

Chapter 12

What are hashtags?

Hashtags have become an invaluable tool for researching certain topics, branding an event, tracking content in a cost-effective way, or building your business brand. A simple way to think of a hashtag is that they are keywords with a # symbol attached to them. So if you've already done your keyword research, then you have done most of the work when it comes to hashtags.

I can't tell you how many times that I personally have used them to connect with people in specific niches of interest. It's now part of my own marketing hack that I include in some of my online marketing strategies that I use for myself and with my clients. If you're not quite sure about using hashtags, I'll share how it can fit into your social business activities on Twitter.

Do's and Don'ts of How To Use Hashtags to Engage

Don't overthink how to use hashtags. They are just additions for finding certain discussions, conferences, and people. For example, if you share articles and blog posts on health and wellness, one hashtag you could use would be #health or #Healthy.

Use hashtags as a way to categorize your content on Twitter and visualize the content that is the most engaging with your community.

Do add you hashtags at the end of your tweets. It is a bit distracting when you see hashtags all over a simple tweet.

Don't add too many hashtags. Depending on what you're tweeting, you may not need more than 3 hashtags. If you are participating in a Twitter chat, try to keep it to one hashtag unless you're mentioning something or someone else.

Do explore hashtags first before you use them. Some hashtags can be linked to spammy tweets, sexbots, or a different industry altogether. You don't want to get blocked on Twitter for the wrong and embarrassing reasons.

Lastly, don't abuse hashtags. Every tweet doesn't have to have a hashtag attached to it. Twitter's search feature is more than capable of finding content that is not connected to a hashtag.

Finding industry-related hashtags can be a cumbersome process. And, if you don't have the time to do the work yourself, having a social media professional like myself can help speed up the process.

Finding Hashtags To Collaborate

Looking for hashtags for whatever your Twitter needs are can be a bit cumbersome at first. Once you know where to look and how to find them, the process becomes less time consuming and a simple thing to do for tweeting.

In another section, I discuss knowing your keywords. When you are familiar with your industry and audience jargon, you can pull certain keywords that can also be the hashtags that you need to follow that will connect you with others. Add a hashtag to those keywords and begin searching the newsfeed for the conversation around those words.

There are websites that you can use to find relevant hashtags that I do mention in Module 4 of the book in Chapter 14. Fast forward for more information about those websites.

Trade Show, Event, and Conference Hashtags

Try using event and conference hashtags to connect around a common core interest because doing this can be mutually beneficial for everyone involved. Finding a hashtag that serves a special target audience being used on Twitter will be even more valuable to you and your business. Make a list of all the useful hashtags and over time continue to follow people who are using them.

MODULE 3
CREATING A SUPER SIMPLE STRATEGY

Chapter 13

6 Step Roadmap For Twitter Success

1 - Set Your Primary Twitter Objectives

You might be wondering what does my business objectives have to do with my Twitter strategy? It has everything to do with your strategy if you don't know where you want to go and how will you get there. How can Twitter fit into your overall marketing strategy if you unaware of your business objectives? You need to understand the activities that you need to get accomplished to meet your business objectives.

What are your business or organization objectives? They are what you want to achieve (the outcomes) from your business strategy. If I were to ask you what results are you wanting to obtain from any set of activities these would be your objectives. Your objectives are what you are striving to achieve.

Once you have decided on your objectives, you need to provide a time a frame for which you will meet your objectives. For example, you want to increase your email opt-in by 10% (about 15 new email leads), this needs to be done in 15 days from the start of the campaign.

Having a schedule that you can abide by will be most beneficial for you if you're an entrepreneur/freelance or marketer for an organization. When you have decided on your measurable objective, creating your budget will help with the upcoming steps on this Twitter roadmap.

The type of organization, your business plan, and overall marketing strategy will dictate your objectives for using Twitter. Here are approximately 11 main objectives you can have for using Twitter which I will share with you today.

1. Lead Generation
2. Increasing brand awareness
3. Increasing website traffic
4. Increase engagement on Twitter
5. Build Thought Leadership
6. Increase sales
7. Increase in content reach and community engagement
8. Nurture and develop relationships with strategic alliances
9. Increase email sign-ups
10. Improve customer service and retention
11. Find employee candidates, mentors, or mentorships

Twitter Activity Questions

1. What are your Twitter objectives?
2. When do you want to accomplish those goals?
3. Do you have the budget to help achieve your Twitter campaign success?

2 - Plan For Finding Your Audience On Twitter

Twitter is a 335 million person melting pot with people from around the world. How will you connect with them on Twitter? In Chapter 4, we discussed your target audience. Now that you have an idea of your target audience, it's time to find them and connect.

Use your keywords. By now you should have a list of your initial keywords that you will use on Twitter. Those keywords when typed into search will enable you to find and listen in on conversations and see the different types of engaging content.

Will you be connecting with competitors and their followers? Or, will you go the route of industry professions and use their key terms? Create about 5 private Twitter lists including the names of industry leaders, industry competitors, engagers, industry associations, and communities. As you start connecting with people, begin to add them to your list so you can begin building relationships and a solid community. Over time keep adding people since some will leave Twitter, others don't tweet often, and there will be about 5-7% (this is based on personal data) who will remain active all the time. If you keep going over time, some people will turn into ambassadors, other business alliances, and some potential clients.

Lastly, make your content copy specifically for your audience. Simple tweaks to your tweet's copy will draw in your ideal audiences. For example, if you are reaching executives you may tweet: "Executives: Are you having trouble keeping your good supervisors at the company? Here are some tips to have a better retention rate." The better you are at creating specific content, the greater the chances of finding your audience on Twitter. Keep going to the next section where I will discuss your content strategy.

Twitter Activity Questions

1. Have you written out your list of keywords?

2. Did you create your Twitter list of people to connect with?
3. Are your strategies working to help you find your audience?

3 - What Does Your Content Strategy Look Like

What kinds of content will you share on Twitter? Before you start creating brand new content, think about the content that you can repurpose for the network . Do you have a podcast, blog, or an active YouTube account? If you have these forms of the content, you have content that you can start sharing on the platform. Keep in mind that you will also need to create or curate content that is appropriate for your objectives. It can not just be random and entertaining content for the sake of content. Motivational quotes are commonly shared and garner retweets but they don't help you build thought leadership or move people to sign up for opt-ins into your sales funnel.

For example, if your objectives are to build influence and become a thought leader, sharing meaningful content that shares your expertise will help you to meet your objective . This content can be an interview in either video and audio format or an article mentioning you. Any content that can tell a story and draws other into you and your mission.

Another question you should ask yourself is how often are you creating original content that you can share with your target audience. If it's not enough, where will you curate content your audience will find useful? Do you have the budget to outsource the writing if you can not do it on a regular basis?

This strategy is not about making things more difficult for you, but it is about using what you have and customizing it for Twitter.

Plan for posting and sharing

How often should you share content on Twitter? It really depends on a number of factors. As a general rule of thumb on any account should be to tweet 3-5 times a day. The average lifespan of a tweet is approximately 30 minutes. The more followers you have or your followers have, the greater the probability that your tweets will not be seen. To avoid this from happening, I recommend you tweet more often. Take a look at your resources. Can you manually tweet or do you need to use a tool or outsource it? What you are able to do is completely up to your situation.

If you're sharing blog content once a day on Twitter, this can work for your needs. But, if one of your objectives is to increase your website traffic, then tweeting a variety of blogs per day is the course of action. When sharing blog posts, it is best to have 2-3 different headline copy for the same blog post so your community doesn't develop content fatigue from your account.

4 - Engagement Plan

You've figured out what are your objectives for Twitter. You know your target audience. You've decided on the best content to create or curate for your target audience. How do you go about getting engagement when you need to help the algorithm work in your favor?

Now it's time to decide what will you do to initiate conversations on Twitter. Will you join Twitter chats? If so, which ones and how often can you participate? Will you create your own Twitter chat? Will you be able to host it, find a partner, pay someone to host the chat, and manage it for you? You will also have to decide how to engage influencers and the strategic relationships you need to have to get the awareness that you need on Twitter.

While you are considering the possibilities, you need to consider how much time can you afford to invest in your engagement plan. If you don't have the time, you need to pay for the resources to make it happen.

The notifications tab will be your best friend. In this section, you should check your notifications often to see who is mentioning you on Twitter. On this tab, you can also see the content that is getting retweeted and favorited.

By now, I'm sure you're tired of hearing me say that Twitter is a social media network and being on the platform is about being social. For anyone who appears in your notifications, you should take time to thank them for sharing, ask them questions, and be social. You can even use this time to move a potential friendly conversation into the DM to see where it can go.

Twitter Activity Questions

1. What types of activities will you participate in?
2. How much time do you have to invest in engaging with others on Twitter?
3. What resources will you use to keep the engagement plan going?

5 - Social Tools For Listening & Managing Twitter

Are you a one man army? If so, then your resources are limited and you may be in the position where you're solely responsible for posting, scheduling and engaging on Twitter. This task can be overwhelming and quite tiring when you have other marketing and outreach duties. This is where tools like Hootsuite, Buffer, Socialoomph, or Sprout Social can help you . Now there are a few more Twitter tools that exist that can help you to schedule content, do your research and select the best tool for you .

As you grow your followers on Twitter it becomes more difficult to listen to every single person and to know what is going on with them. Social listening tools allow you to create groups of people and place them in a stream to follow the content of others. Keeping an ear to the social network offers you the opportunity to find ways to inject yourself into the conversation or listen for when someone @mentions you.

Are you part of a medium to a large organization? Your technological needs will vary and are determined based on the needs of the company. You may need an enterprise level support or a social tool that can offer in depth analysis more frequently than the average social tool.

Twitter Activity Questions

1. Do you need a Twitter tool for one person team or an enterprise level?

2. How much can you allot to maintaining this tool on a regular basis?
3. What kind of features do you need that is non-negotiable?

6 - T.E.A. Time (Measure Your Findings)

In order to know what is working on Twitter, you will need to track your metrics. Most people don't even know that they have access to so much information that can be found on Twitter analytics. Use Twitter analytics to measure the effectiveness of your actions, but any tool that can provide you with metrics to assess your Twitter activity will be sufficient.

Test

Test everything. Test how many tweets is the most beneficial for the objectives you've created. Increase or , decrease the number of times that you tweet. Change the times that you tweet. If you normally do it in the morning, try the evening and vice versa. Test the days of the week and how often you tweet on certain days. Test the content you share and try sharing content out of the box.

Edit

Based on what you discover from the testing you've done, it is wise to make adjustments and edit as necessary. You might need to change keywords or use a particular word. Edit your tweet's copy. Maybe your title is off-putting and could be turning your audience away from your brand. The point is to figure out what is working and optimize it to make it better. Don't focus on what is not working for you.

Analyze

It is paramount that you constantly assess what is working on Twitter. This includes the types of content, when you engage, what times you engage, and the copy of the posts. This is the only way that you can pivot if the content and engagement strategy is not working. Figuring out what triggers your community to respond should always be on your mind so that you can recreate more of those content pieces.

Twitter has free analytics that anyone can use as long as you have an account. The information they provide is almost the same information that Facebook has on their dashboard. Go here https://analytics.twitter.com to check on the various Twitter metrics important to your organization. (Please note that you may need to open your ads account in order to see your data.))

Twitter Metrics To Track

Do you know what metrics to consider when doing a campaign using Twitter? The more you know about your audience, their interest, and what type of content causes them to respond, the better you will be able to customize your tactics for success. There are a few metrics you will want to keep in mind when you are analyzing your content.

1. **Tweets**: How many tweets have you sent in a given time? Do you need to increase or decrease tweets?

2. **Tweet Impressions:** Are you getting into the Twitter timeline of the people you're attempting to connect with?

3. **Profile Visits:** Is your community showing interest in you?

4. **Mentions:** Are you being mentioned? Have your mentions increased or decreased? Can you see any correlations to the other metrics?

5. **Followers:** Is your Twitter strategy working to grow your followers and community of an ideal audience?

6. **Audience:** Within the audience information you can tell who is following you and what is their interest.

Below are images of the main twitter analytics tab and the audience tab.

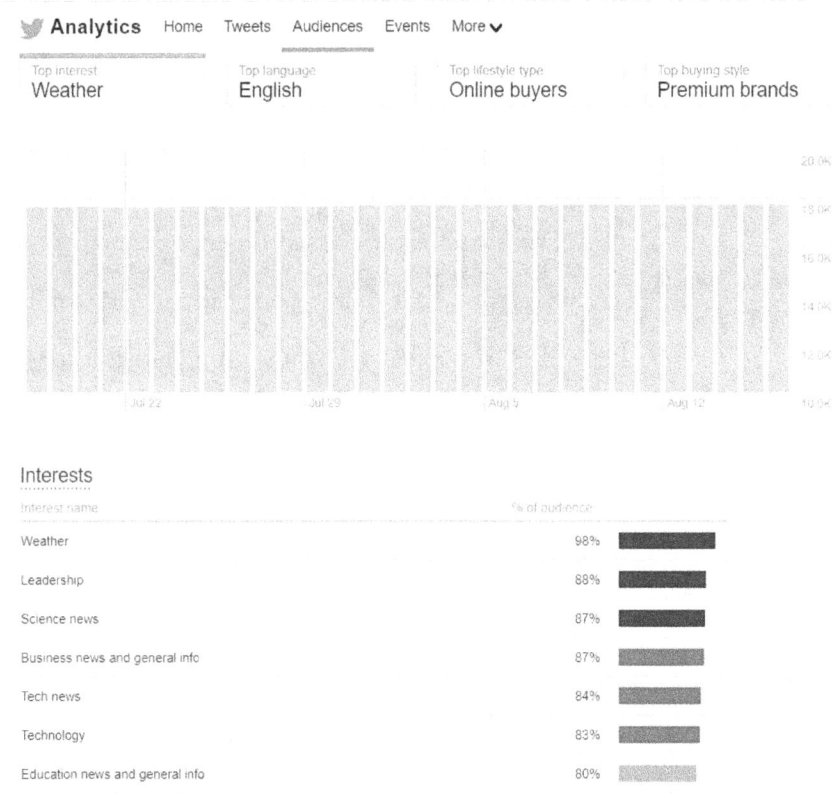

28 day summary with change over previous period

Tweets	Tweet impressions	Profile visits	Mentions	Followers
377 ↑18.6%	86.8K ↓6.7%	1,472 ↑36.5%	329 ↑41.8%	17.8K ↑105

Twitter Activity Questions

1. What types of content have you been sharing and what were your findings?
2. What will you change based on your recent assessment?
3. What is the next thing you will try or won't try on Twitter? And, what are you wanting to achieve?
4. What metrics are the most valuable for the current campaign?

Module 4
Using technology:
Twitter Tools and Resources

Chapter 14

Tools Time

Tools serve a purpose and their purpose is to make your life and job easier to handle. Don't fall for the shiny object syndrome when you are approaching the topics of tools. Find a handful of tools that will help propel you forward in your business. Implement one tool at a time and figure out as many features as possible.

Twitter Search

Twitter search is very basic, but quite valuable for finding almost anything piece of information that has been posted to Twitter. All of the information you could possibly need is at the touch of the button. When you're trying to find your target audience, I recommend this tool to do your research . There are times I don't have time to pull open my other search tool.

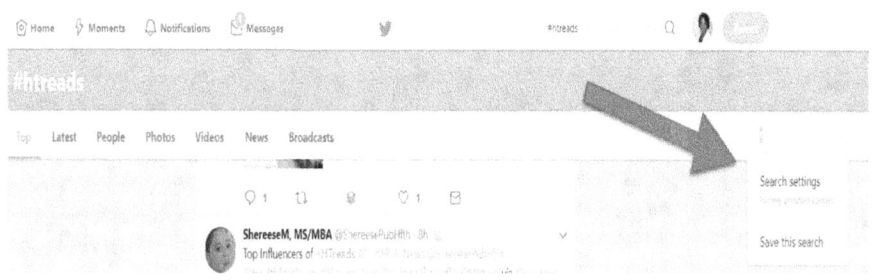

Twitter Advanced Search

Take your research up a notch by using Twitter's advanced search features. Similar to the regular search feature, you are capable of finding real-time conversations with the information you've inputted into advanced search tool.

Here's the direct link: https://twitter.com/search-advanced

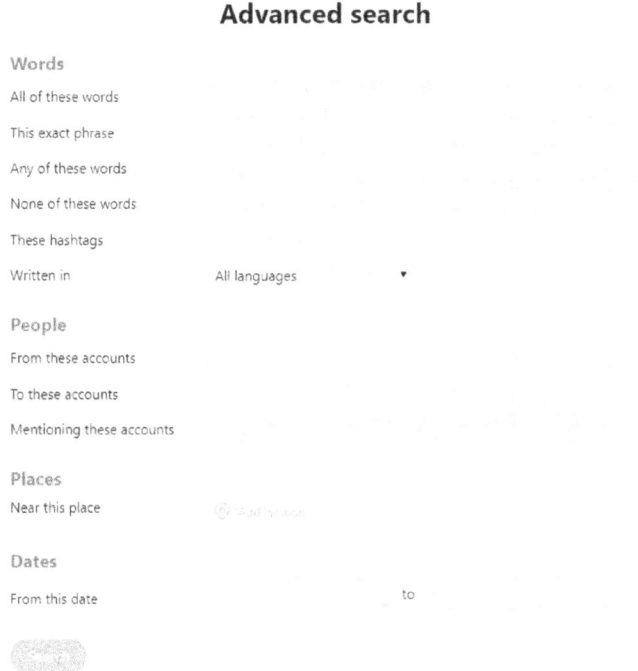

Hootsuite

Hootsuite was one of my first tools and is a favorite of mine. It's a social media management and listening tool that's free unless you're managing more than 5 accounts. After you exceed that limit, you would need to upgrade your account. It is capable of handling the top social media networks except Snapchat. Not only can it handle multiple social networks, but it is great for handling multiple accounts for different people. If you manage social media accounts like my company does, it's a great option with a fairly decent investment.

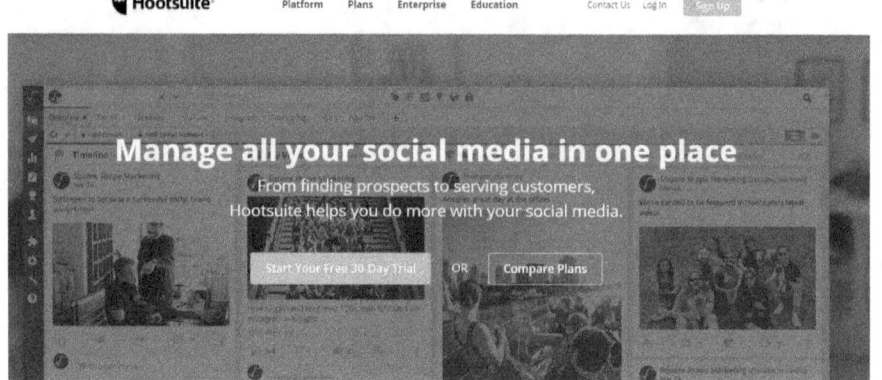

Trusted by 800+ of the Fortune 1000

TweetDeck

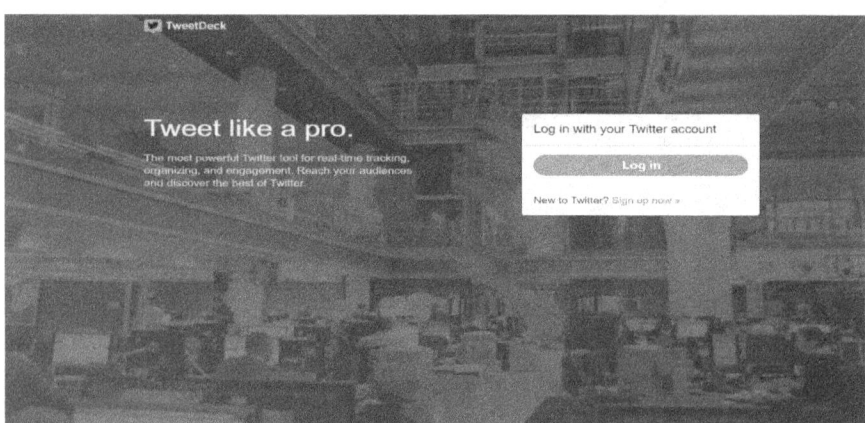

Never miss a tweet with Tweetdeck. Follow your list, twitter stream, schedule, and post them all from this platform. Tweetdeck is only a desktop tool that is now owned by Twitter and has a great user interface. It has many features to offer so you should consider going to the website and checking them out. I'll be sharing just a few of the features here. Like Socialoomph, you can schedule tweets, but it doesn't have a way to store your evergreen content. If you have a virtual assistant or someone that handles your Twitter account, the great thing about Tweetdeck is that you can provide them access on the platform without actually giving them your Twitter password. Did I mention that Tweetdeck is a completely free tool to use? There is no paid option as of 2018.

Tchat.io

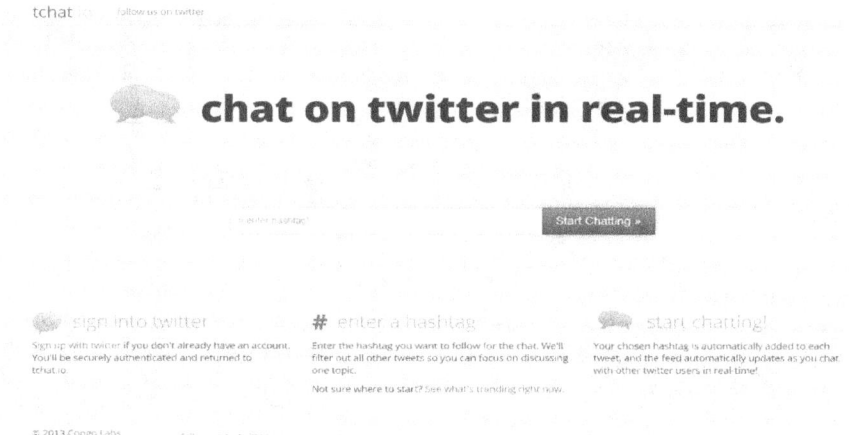

Tchat.io is a tool to help you follow along twitter chats, events, or conversation with a hashtag. It's a great platform that is simple to use and you don't have to worry about adding hashtags to the conversation. Try it because it doesn't get any simpler than this dashboard.

Symplur

This social media tool serves many purposes, but we will focus on the fact that they are valuable at curating hashtags in the healthcare industry and providing analytical reports for Twitter.

ManageFlitter:

Clean up your Twitter list of inactive and fake followers with ManageFlitter. This is a free bulk follow/unfollow tool with limitation and Pro features with all access. This is the tool I used to cleanup my account when I hit my Twitter limit. Today I still use the platform for it useful Twitter search dashboard and the ability to sort through my own followers.

Phone Apps To Download

Twitter Native App

The main app that I use on my phone for tweeting on the go is the Twitter native app. I use emojis on quite a few of my tweets so having direct access on Twitter to share them cuts down on the time I need to find them. The native app obviously is free and gets updated when something new is added. In general, there are hardly any glitches and it's one of the most realizable social apps.

Hootsuite/Buffer app

These two apps are the best for sharing and scheduling content on the go which is necessary when you are a team of 5 or less. The Hootsuite app and Buffer app allow me to schedule content later if I've been engaging in real time and I don't want to over flood my Twitter timeline. You can't always carry around your laptop and don't always have access to your desktop. These apps are free with the option to upgrade to the pro version.

Chapter 15

Automation Is Your Virtual Assistant

Automation seems like a dirty word in business, but this is a hot discussion topic for many small business owners and entrepreneurs. Automation tools are either recommended or are not considered to be a business necessity. Twitter automation tools are needed so that you can keep a consistent presence online while you do other money-making activities for you business. Let's face it. To run a successful business, you can't spend all day and night following people, tweeting, retweeting, and engaging in conversations unless that is part of your business model. And, for most of us that is not the case. When you use the right tools, it's like having a personal VA for your Twitter account. There are quite a few helpful desktop tools and apps that I use in my everyday day routine that I highly recommend for you.

Why You Need To Use It

Why do you need an assistant? An assistant is there to provide you support for certain tasks in order to help you accomplish more hands-on activities that only you can do. Right? Well, any type of tool whether it is for social listening or social automation, is there to do the same things. An automation tool allows you to share general content to Twitter so that you can actively engage without wondering if you have provided any value or shared that opt-in. Maybe you're planning a vacation, you don't want your account to be vacant if you are going offline for a week. Staying active on Twitter in addition to another network can get complicated so you need better ways to make sure that you are posting content on each network.

What To Remember About Using Automation

Automation is there to make your life more productive and manageable. There will always be people who are willing to disagree that you as an individual shouldn't use it because it's a tool for larger organization, but that is not the case.

Use an automation tool to help streamline certain activities that can be redundant like scheduling blog posts. Upcoming announcements for events, new services, books, apps, and product launches should be scheduled in advance. This gives you time to engage in real-time conversations. Don't get lazy with engaging on Twitter because you have tweets scheduled. Any automation is not to be used as a replacement for real-time conversations or to spam people in their DMs.

Module 5
Protect Ya Neck

Chapter 16

Protecting Yourself, The consumer, and Your Business

Did you know that Twitter.com has one of the highest page ranks on Google? It is considered an authority site and has a pagerank of 10.

If you have an abandoned your Twitter account, knowing that your profile could rank high on Google just for being active on this social network should be enough to bring you back and bring life to your Twitter account.

The stronger your search presence, the more difficult it is for someone to slander your brand. Finding a way to link your social media accounts to Twitter is great for building an online Twitter reputation. Remember that an online reputation takes time and energy to build.

What is Reputation Management?

Online reputation management encompasses so many things. Many times we think of online reputation management or ORM as a process we go through when the public brand needs to repair a negative situation that has occurred. ORM is a collection of building an online brand reputation, monitoring your brand, repairing both reactively and proactively, and lastly protecting your reputation.

Your Twitter reputation is part of the equation and needs to guarded scrupulously with a wide eye. On a fast-paced social network like Twitter, it can be quite easy to let your guard down and believe no one is paying you any attention. Let me tell you, lurkers are the biggest population on the platform and are constantly watching regardless of whether they favorite, reply, or retweet your content. This means that your Twitter reputation is always vulnerable and should be monitored and protected at all cost.

How To Manage Your Online Twitter Reputation

I mentioned earlier that your Twitter reputation will be stronger when linked to your other social media accounts. How can you link your accounts when you are only given one location to put your web address? Networks like Facebook and LinkedIn allow you to connect your Twitter account within their own profile settings. Don't miss out on these simple opportunities to share your Twitter info plus add a few layers to your online reputation.

The things you tweet about today can haunt you in 5,10,15 years from now. And, understanding that your tweets can be indexed on Google is an even greater reason to be mindful of what you choose to share and discuss on the network.

Your Privacy Options

If you are wanting to build authority within your industry as a brand or business, having a public profile is the way you want to go. That is why it is crucial to know what are your long-term goals and objectives for being on Twitter and social media in general. If you have any type of business, whether full time or a side hustle, you will want to determine the benefits of having a private account vs. a public account.

Protected Account (Private)

A protected Twitter account cannot be indexed on Google and therefore it will be considered unlisted. The general public will not be able to see your Twitter content unless you follow them. Twitter will let them know that the account is private and they will have to follow you to see your tweets.

This option works if you do not want to found on Google and if you are not trying to build your brand on Twitter. Remember that even though your account is private, someone who follows you can still screenshot your tweets if you are connected and can share it on Twitter as a picture. Make sure the people you choose to connect with on a private account are trustworthy.

Here are few things to consider even when you have a protected account:

- Adding your employer's name on your profile can be seen.
- Incorporating any potential info in your bio which can be misconstrued by an outsider reading your profile information.
- Don't add an offensive profile image
- Anonymous tweets can be traced back to you with the right software.

Public Account

Are you trying to grow your brand influence, business, product, app, or service visibility? Then you will want to have a public and active Twitter account. There is just no way around it. You need this especially in

2018. You don't exist if someone cannot find you on Twitter. Remember that I said this!

Use Twitter to create an authoritative account that will rank high on Google that will increase your chances of being in the first 10 listings when someone googles your name, brand, or business. Before you post to Twitter, think first and tweet later. Would you say this exact tweet with someone you have never met before? If your answer is no, then don't share it on Twitter. Be mindful of what you post. Are your tweets outright offensive? Use common sense and don't hide behind the social network.

Should You Have Two Twitter Accounts?

Having two Twitter accounts can work to your benefit especially if you have a professional career and a side business or for your personal connections and building your online brand. You do not want to create a jumbled brand presence that could catch up with you in a negative way later.

I am not here to tell you if you should or should not have two accounts without first knowing your short-term or long-term goals. But, I can tell you that if you have any type of business, the time to start growing your account is years before you actually need it. Twitter is a long-term tactic. Although your reputation on Twitter can be destroyed within hours, it can take months to years to create a reputation worth sharing with others.

Key Things To Remember To Protect Your Online Twitter Reputation

- Be respectful at all times even when the situation turns sour.

- Be honest and refrain from using false names (unless this is a personal account)

- In Twitter, disagreements may happen, so remain polite and behave diplomatically. Don't be too quick to engage or disengage in the conversation.

- When in doubt, refer to your legal, Human Resource, or PR team.

- Don't engage trolls

- Be quick to apologize when necessary. Be even quicker to listen first to make sure you understand the tweet before you engage.

- Remain true to your brand message, mission, and tone.

- Understand that you are responsible for your brand and what gets communicated on the network.

Chapter 17

Do you have a Twitter Policy?

Do you have a way to protect your business, organization, employees, and yourself by having a social media policy which includes Twitter in place? If you don't you could be putting all you've worked for at risk and it's time to put one in place.

It's one thing if you're a company of one or two. You are playing a completely different ballgame if you have consultants, freelancers, and employees (full-time or part-time) working with you.

A Twitter policy does not exist by itself, but it will be in conjunction with a social media policy. This chapter will mainly discuss Twitter's role in your policy. Twitter should not be overlooked because it may not be the most popular social network. One tweet, 280 characters, carries the ability to jeopardize one's brand reputation and in the blink of an eye make your organization become the #1 enemy.

Don't let that happen due to the ignorance of your staff because they unknowingly shared information in error. Empower your organization by making sure they are aware of what they can and can not post to Twitter.

This section's purpose is not to give you a Twitter policy, but is here as a reminder that if you don't have one to get one created ASAP . And, if there is one, make sure your organization is thoroughly aware of the Do's & Don'ts and what information might get them fired from their position or even sued.

Understanding Company Policy

Be proactive and not reactive! Do you need to completely prohibit the use of Twitter by your staff? This is a touchy subject that is best determined by the needs of your organization. Every organization has its own extenuating circumstances To increase the productivity and alleviate the number of distractions, some organizations have added firewalls on the internet to prevent access to social media networks.

Personally, I believe there is a time and place for your staff to use Twitter that could be detrimental to the online health of your organization. There needs to be a level of authenticity and transparency online. By allowing your staff to be brand ambassadors, this can only work towards your organization's digital footprint success. Why not harness the power of Twitter to create an open dialogue and engage with potential audiences that want to know about your organization? Be flexible with the idea of using the network as a potential customer service gateway for current consumers and all stakeholders.

Your organization's Twitter policy should include a few things:

- ❏ Goals of any social media activities by the potential staff
- ❏ Scenarios surrounding "how" social media can be used that is beneficial to the organizations
- ❏ Guidelines of the content that the staff can share on their personal profiles without breaking the organizational policy.
- ❏ Visual content guide. (approved images, gifs, video, live streams)

- ❏ Offer acceptable copy and past disclaimers the staff can use in their bio profile.

- ❏ Customer service do's and don'ts about what can be answered online. (If your organization uses this as a means for open communications with current consumers)

- ❏ Information that is considered offensive, goes against the code of conduct or values, and could lead to termination .

- ❏ The course of action that should be taken in case of a communication mishap.

- ❏ Who the staff member should contact in case of questions about the Twitter policy.

- ❏ A cheat sheet that is available for staff to have on hand

Your policies and guidelines should continually evolve as the network and the organizational usages evolve. Take time to make sure that everything is up to date. Initially, it will seem like a waste of time, but ensure that all staff goes through the Twitter policy everytime it gets an update. This is your best offensive strategy for preventing future dilemmas.

Do Your Employees Know The Rules

When was was the last time your HR department has gone over with your staff about the Twitter policy? If your organization is not big enough to have HR, have you gone over the rules of employees using Twitter? Just because you don't have an HR department does not exclude you from making sure everyone is knowing and understanding about any potential issues arising from their use on the platform.

Don't assume that because you made everyone sign a copy of the rules, it means that it was read. I know from working at an organization for years that I couldn't describe to you anything about their social media policy. I just signed what they told me to sign and went about performing my duties. In general, I am cautious of what I posted to Twitter just because I was unsure of the actual terms. But, with Twitter becoming mainstream, people are sharing more candidly and these Twitter moments can go against the policy. Make sure your staff is aware of the policies that exist about Twitter and social media, in general. Create time to have a meeting about company expectations about online activities and to answer any questions. Provide ongoing and necessary training to your staff who are handling your social accounts. Twitter is constantly changing and keeping update is just another needed responsibility. Don't shy away from protecting what you've worked so hard to build and everyone involved.

Final Thoughts: Twitter Marketing Unlocked

I did a podcast interview with [Deepa Shukla](), and he said it best. "We have to remember that there is a human behind that tweet." Sometimes it's easy to forget that it is a person tweeting and they are human just like us. It's too easy to forget that we need to humanize our brand by building valued connections on a platform like Twitter when we have business or organizational objectives.

Thank you for taking the time to purchase my book! I hope you were able to walk away knowing a little more about Twitter than you did before you picked up this book. The best thing about Twitter is that while everyone is running over to Instagram, there is still white space and room to grow on the network. Organic reach, organic connections, and organic brand visibility are very much alive with some work on your part.

Keep remembering that Twitter is the lowest hanging fruit when it comes to connecting with others on the network. Be open to meeting new people and become uncomfortable with jumping into conversations with random strangers. That is one the best parts of being on Twitter afterall. Start communicating in public, take it private to a dm or private message, and when possible take the conversations to some offline communication. In most cases, taking the relationship to a deeper level is the goal of most when using social networks like Twitter for business.

Don't be afraid to experiment on the network because different strategies will work differently depending on your industry. If anyone tells you that your business is too visual for Twitter, don't believe them. In fact, that would be your competitive edge. Anything that can make you stand out will be welcomed on this social network.

If you've made it to the end of the book, congratulations! Please reach out to me and let me know that you have made it to end and what you think about the book.

Keep at it and Happy Tweeting!

ABOUT THE AUTHOR

Angela Hemans holds a bachelor's degree in Business Administration from Saint Leo University. Her background includes helping patients as a cardiovascular sonographer, but her passion for entrepreneurs and entrepreneurship has led her to diagnostics of a different sort.

Angela founded the Women United in Business Mastermind Group to facilitate networking and experience-sharing, and she enjoys working with business professionals and authors from diverse industries and backgrounds to develop and implement tailored sales solutions. She helps professionals establish an online presence or platform that enhances their brand through social media and marketing communications and helps them improve social media and networking skills.

Angela's insight and know-how helps businesses, consultants, nonprofits, start-ups and authors establish themselves within their professional industry and among their online communities.

Connect With Me On Social Media

https://twitter.com/AngelaHemans

https://www.linkedin.com/in/angelahemans/

https://www.pinterest.com/angelahemans/

https://www.facebook.com/theangelahemans/

http://www.angelahemans.com/

www.ingramcontent.com/pod-product-compliance
Lightning Source LLC
Chambersburg PA
CBHW071411220526
45469CB00004B/1249